THE
UNDISCOVERED
CHRIST

THE UNDISCOVERED CHRIST

MARK JOHN CHIRONNA

Destiny Image Publishers
P.O. Box 310
Shippensburg, PA 17257-0310

"Speaking to the Purposes of God for this Generation"

ISBN 1-56043-085-0

For Worldwide Distribution
Printed in the U.S.A.

DEDICATION

This book is dedicated to my wife Ruth, who has taught me to appreciate what Christ has done for me in my life. It is also dedicated to my sons Matthew and Daniel, who are God's promise to me that a new generation can be birthed in the glory of God.

Finally, this book is dedicated to the people of Higher Call Christian Center, the local church where I pastor, for they have convinced me by their lives that there is a generation that hungers and thirsts after the fullness of Christ.

Mark J. Chironna

CONTENTS

FOREWORD

In my late teens, I became increasingly aware of the call of God in my life. Once I submitted myself to God's purposes, one particular scripture became an anchor of my life and ministry. The words of the Apostle Paul which I memorized were something like this: "I strive to preach the Gospel not where Jesus has already been named, lest I should build upon another man's foundation."

After 40 years of full-time ministry, as I reflected on that same passage of scripture, I was amazed to discover that I had been reading the verse incorrectly! It does not say, "where *Jesus* has been named;" it says, "where *Christ* has been named."

Don't minsunderstand what I am suggesting here. I do not minimize the name of *Jesus*. Certainly,

Jesus is fundamental to salvation. In *Jesus* rests all of redemption. But there must come a time when individual Christians, local churches and the Body of Christ at large come into a fuller revelation of *the Christ*. Coming to know *the Christ* is by divine revelation.

It is the revelation of Jesus as *the Christ* that will cause the Church and the Gospel of the Kingdom to become headline news in the 21st century! God is in the business of raising up a generation of believers who will not only declare the Gospel in demonstrations of power, but will storm the very gates of hell. These God-called men and women will arise out of the decay of the inner-cities of America and will turn their generation toward God. The voices of the forerunners of this movement are already beginning to be heard. Mark Chironna—the author of this book—is one of them.

The Undiscovered Christ is a forerunner book— many more volumes by many other authors will follow and will herald the Gospel in the 21st century. This book introduces an emphasis upon *the Christ* which must be recognized throughout the Body of Christ as a primary revelation that the Holy Spirit is manifesting in this rising generation.

The spiritual insight to write the following pages could only have come through times of prolonged communion with God—by abiding in His Word and in His presence. As you read *The Undiscovered Christ* I can promise you one thing: A hunger will be put in your heart and you will yearn to know *the Christ* in a deeper and fuller revelation than you have yet known Him.

Bishop John L. Meares
Evangel Church
Upper Marlboro, Maryland

CHAPTER ONE

THE UNDISCOVERED CHRIST

To make a statement that, for most of us, Christ is undiscovered could seem somewhat scandalous at the outset. Yet in actuality, we must admit that there is much about Him we have yet to discover; there is much about Him that as yet remains hidden from us. Our whole basis for life is wrapped up in knowing Him. Eternal life, by Jesus' own definition, is to know Him (John 17:2). In the same way, without a knowledge of Christ, the Church cannot live in the scriptural reality of hope. Hope is realized in the person of Christ. Christ in us is the hope of glory!

In Matthew 13:44, Jesus speaks parabolically of the pearl of great price. One can interpret that verse in many dimensions. Yet for the purpose of our consideration, let's imagine that it speaks of the indwelling Christ. The parable lets us know a number of things. In order to acquire the pearl, one must personally renounce whatever else had worth prior to the pearl's discovery. Secondly, one cannot make immediate use of the pearl; therefore, it must remain hidden until all other affairs are put in order and until one discerns the true purpose of such a valuable treasure. Thirdly, if the pearl did not cost its discoverer a very high price, that individual would esteem the treasure lightly and, as a result, defile it.

How many times have we lightly esteemed the One who indwells the Church and, without realizing it, "cast our pearls before swine"? Isn't it true that when we acted out of our own uncontrolled ambitions, we lost the pearl, or more specifically, we lost the revelation of His indwelling?

Matthew 11:27 declares:

All things have been handed over to Me by My Father; and no one knows the Son, except the Father; nor does anyone know the Father, except the Son, and anyone to whom the Son wills to reveal Him.

2

Immediately and painfully we are made aware of the fact that there is a knowledge exclusive in God, to which man in his own efforts or even by good works cannot attain. In essence, Christ remains UNDISCOVERED (unless the Father reveals Him to an individual). We can be raised in a Christian environment, observe all the rules and regulations of our particular denomination or non-denomination, appease our conscience by much religious activity, and still not KNOW CHRIST. Yes, we can be born again, converted, even Spirit-baptized, and still be ignorant of Him who dwells in the Church. John the Baptist made a statement which in some ways still applies to the modern church: "...among you stands One whom you do not know" (John 1:26).

What is required to know this One? In the text of Matthew 11, Jesus declares that the Father has hidden things from the wise and from the intelligent (v. 25). The wise and the intelligent are those who assume they know. These are also the same ones addressed as the weary and heavy-laden in verse 28. Accumulated knowledge is no guarantee of wholeness. As a matter of fact, often times the more knowledge one gains, the more pain one endures. The knowledge of Christ is an experience. It does not come by sweat and effort; rather it comes by revelation from the hand of a God who in His wisdom hides the pearl from people whose preoccupations keep them from searching for the hidden meaning of life. They are far too caught up in acquiring other things to appreciate the pearl of great price.

God has given to every child of His the ability to hear His voice, but many times in our lives we fail to listen, and thus forfeit the pearl. So the pearl remains hidden and undiscovered. The Christ of glory lies deep within the spirit of the believer and the community of God. Yet for one reason or another, whether we have become numb to our hunger or preoccupied with other pursuits, He remains the undiscovered treasure in each of us.

In the first three chapters of Revelation, Jesus repeats a phrase at the end of every address that He delivers to the seven churches of Asia Minor. That phrase is "he who has an ear, let him hear." Notice also, in your meditations of these three chapters, that apparently the only ones who overcome in each church are those who listen. It is possible to have the auditory faculty of spiritual ears and yet ignore what is being heard. To discover the undiscovered, indwelling Christ requires a unique interchange and dialogue between God and us. Dialogue with the One first requires that I open the door when He knocks (Rev. 3:20), and then invite Him to enter and speak. "Speak, for Thy servant is listening" (1 Sam 3:10).

4

The knowledge of the Son is hidden in the Father. Only the Father knows the Son perfectly. In Matthew 16, that great chapter where Peter makes the grand confession of "Thou art the Christ...." Jesus faces the culmination of His earthly journey and work. His burden and concern is for His disciples to have an accurate perception of who He truly is. Jesus is quite aware that the multitudes have no conception at all of that knowledge. His passion is for those who were with Him from the beginning to know who He truly is.

Therefore Jesus raises questions to draw from the disciples what they are thinking. He first asks, "Who do people say that the Son of Man is?"(v. 13). The disciples go through a list of a few significant individuals in covenant history. Each of those mentioned were mightily used of God. However, none of those perceptions, whether they said Jesus was Elijah, Jeremiah, Isaiah or whoever, was an accurate perception. He then asks, on a personal note, "Who do YOU SAY I am?" (v. 15 NIV). Simon Peter responds for the rest and says, "Thou art the Christ, the Son of the living God" (v. 16). Jesus lauds the answer given by Simon Peter and blesses him. He then makes it quite clear that Simon Peter's seeing Jesus the Man was "the Christ" required an encounter with the Father, who alone reveals the Son, not flesh and blood. The Hebrew

5

concept of "flesh and blood" concerns human agencies that perhaps would have taught religious systems of truth to the community of Israel. In other words, it means the rabbis or the priests. Obviously the knowledge Simon Peter had would not have come from that arena, for Christ was fully hidden by the Father from their view.

Jesus affirmed for Simon Peter that the Father was doing an inward work of grace in his heart and was revealing His Son to a hungry fisherman. Jesus also made it clear that what Simon saw was a mystery. When Simon said, "Thou art the Christ," he saw more than the Man, Jesus. Simon saw the ONE of whom John the Baptist said, "After me comes a Man who has a higher rank than I, for He existed before me" (John 1:30). Simon saw the Pre-existent One veiled in a human body. At least, he had caught enough of a glimpse of Him to make the right declaration of what he saw. That is ESSENTIAL revelation. Movement toward destiny cannot be made without first establishing that essential revelation in the spirit of man.

Jesus, the Son of Mary, is the Christ. He was the eternal One who met Moses at the burning bush and who appeared to him in glory on Sinai. He is the One who appeared to Abraham at the oaks of Mamre to assure him that Sarah would bear a son. Simon, by revelation of the Father, saw that this

Jesus was the One with whom Jacob had wrestled all night long. This One appeared in the fiery furnace with the three Hebrew children. This same Jesus, in His pre-existence, was seen by Isaiah as high and lifted up.

There is one thing we must be careful of, however. We often refer to the appearances of the pre-incarnate Son of God in the Old Testament as appearances of Jesus. The Son of God did not become Jesus, Mary's boy-child, until the Incarnation. It is important to understand this concept because Jesus, the Man, did not exist until He was born of Mary's womb. Yet Christ, the Son of the living God, pre-dates time and space. He is eternal. Isaiah says, "For unto us a child is born [that is, Jesus], unto us a son is GIVEN [that is, Christ]" (9:6 KJV). There is a difference because the Son of God was given, not BORN! The Son of God became Jesus the Man at His earthly birth. He took on human nature and a human name. As a matter of fact, "Jesus" was a very common name, much like "Jim" or "John" is in our day. However, once the Son of God became man and took the name Jesus, as instructed by Gabriel the angel, that common name became UNCOMMON! Never has a man been born since then, that if their name was Jesus, it almost would seem sacrilegious. He, by His very life and nature, took the common and made it holy!

7

It is this revelation, which can only be given and not obtained, that is the foundation for the building up or edifying of the Church. Actually, there is no Church if there is no Christ. To have an *exkklesia,* a "called out company", there must be a Christ to call them out of the earthly and into the heavenly. Just as Abraham was called out of Ur of the Chaldees as the result of the God of glory appearing to him (Acts 7:2), so was Simon called out of an earthly system of dead works into serving the living God because the God of glory appeared to him in Jesus. Somewhere beyond the veil of the flesh of Jesus, Simon Peter saw the pearl of great price and, as a result, he left everything to follow Him, in order to obtain the pearl and discover its purpose.

Foundational, therefore, to the life of the Church is the revelation of the Son of God. Christ is the Head of a Body. There is indeed a Head, so there must be a Body! When Jesus said He would build His Church upon that rock of revelation, He was making it clear, even there, that the Church was His property. Jesus said that the Church was His personal possession. "I will build MY CHURCH," Jesus said (Matt. 16:18). He thus clearly shows that He is the One who reveals the Father to those whom He chooses, and when He does, the Father reveals the Son to those same individuals. We cannot build the Church, for it has not been given to us to reveal the Father. Only the Son can do that. When the Son reveals the Father, then the Father in turn reveals the Son to those who were given to Him.

Jesus Christ is building His Church. Not only is He building His Church, or His Body (for if there is a Head, there must also be a Body), neither can that which has determined to destroy, namely the gates of hell, intimidate or override this task that Jesus is performing. These gates of hell are councils of princes and powers who sit in places of access (gates) into population centers so they can control what goes in and what comes out. These "gates" are places where alien forces of chaos seek to overthrow the gift of life with a sentence of death. Jesus confidently declares that, as individuals encounter the God of truth and see the undiscovered Christ veiled in Jesus the Man, that which the powers and princes used to deny people access are overturned and places of ascent are manifested which lift the Church from the earthly into the heavenly. The revelation of the Christ leads to an open heaven where angels ascend and descend upon the Son of Man.

CHAPTER TWO

THE UNRELENTING FOE

The phrase "gates of hell" is synonymous with an alien and hostile network of demonic princes that scheme to bring a sentence of death to the revelation of Christ. Gates are always places of access. Gates are portals of entry and of departure. In the ancient eastern world, whoever possessed the gates of a city possessed the city. Elders would sit in the gates and make decisions that concerned the welfare of the city. Part of the promise to Abraham was that his seed would possess the gates of his enemies. Therefore, the promise Jesus made in

Matthew 16:18 seems to refer to the fulfillment of Genesis 22:17, where God made the promise to Abraham.

Dealing with and unmasking the princes and powers is part of the ongoing conflict the Church endures as the revelation of Christ increases. All of hell is bent on preventing that revelation from effectually working in the earth. If the powers can neutralize the Church, they will. Nevertheless, the Master, who conquered this dark and sinister network of malevolent spirits as well as their commander satan, has given us His assurance and His Spirit to totally annihilate these angelic princes, until every enemy is a footstool for the feet of Jesus (Ps. 110:2). From the very beginning there were forces at work, attempting to interfere with the creative process of God. These are the forces of chaos and anti-creation. In the beginning God took the unformed earth from chaos to order. The Spirit of the Lord always moves creation from chaos to order. The alien forces of darkness constantly work to move the creation from order to chaos.

Lies and deception fill the atmosphere to the same degree that pollution fills the natural air over many parts of the world. While in the natural our environment is strewn with toxic debris, the powers of darkness fill the invisible arena with psychic debris. The minds of men are constantly exposed to spiritual toxic waste that is present for the purpose of disuniting and disintegrating the eternal purpose of God.

We must wage effective warfare on a level much higher than perhaps we have comprehended. In the Gulf War of 1991, the level of "high tech" information and weaponry which was at the disposal of the generals in command became evident to the public. It was war on a rather sophisticated level. The Gulf War was fought first in the command control centers, where generals sat to devise strategy and outmaneuver their opponents. In essence, the war was won or lost in the planning stages. The need to gain "air superiority" was uppermost in the minds of the allied effort against Iraq. In similar fashion, it was in the mind of the Lord to gain air superiority over the princes and powers and regain access to the hearts and minds of men and women.

The mind of man is like a city. "He who is slow to anger is better than the mighty, and he who rules his spirit, than he who captures a city" (Prov. 16:32). The Hebrew connotation of "a city" was a collection of permanent human habitations, whether many or few, and especially if surrounded by a wall. The "city of God" refers to the people of God throughout the Scripture. The walls of the city of God are called SALVATION, and the gates of this city are called PRAISE (Is. 60:18). The Church, Mount Zion, is the city of the living God (Heb.

12:22ff.). We are surrounded by the walls of the Lord, even as the mountains surround the natural city of Jerusalem (Ps. 125:2).

This verse in Proverbs seems to imply that if a man can rule his spirit (his inner city), he can capture the city in which he lives. We cannot gain air superiority in our residential cities until we gain air superiority over our internal cities. Our emotions, as well as our appetites and desires, must be under our control. Our minds must be freed from the psychic debris that fills the invisible atmosphere and we must breathe in the air of the heavenly city of God. This warfare cannot be won by simply attacking the demonic around us. Careful planning must take place in the council chambers of Heaven. It is there where the generals of the underworld must be outmaneuvered.

There indeed is a heavenly council. Jeremiah 23:18 makes it evident that without access into that council chamber, one cannot speak on behalf of God. "But who has stood in the COUNCIL of the Lord, that he should SEE and HEAR His word?..." "The anger of the Lord will not turn back until He has performed and carried out the purposes of His heart; in the last days you will clearly understand it" (Jer. 23:20). It is in this council chamber that God gathers His generals to hear and see divine strategies to destroy the powers of darkness which hold sway over the minds of men. The battle for the minds of men must first be won in the war room.

Every solid government of every nation on earth has an INTELLIGENCE DEPARTMENT. The intelligence department is responsible for uncovering, discovering and providing a reasonable degree of secret information that can be used to successfully overcome the opposition. It is the responsibility of the intelligence department to get behind enemy lines without being noticed.

In Scripture it is always the Spirit, catching men up into the council and allowing them to see and hear what goes beyond the natural faculties, that gives the edge to the people of God. One of the clearest examples of this advantage is in Second Kings 6:12, where the Arameans plotted to capture Elisha because they discovered he was intercepting knowledge of enemy activity: "No, my lord, O king; but Elisha, the prophet who is in Israel, tells the king of Israel the words that you speak in your bedroom." Elisha was given access by the Spirit to knowledge that transcended the physical limitations of his existence. In actuality, Elisha stood in the heavenly council and saw and heard things to frustrate the enemies of God.

(Meredith Kline, in his monumental work *Images of the Spirit*, deals at great length with the issue of the heavenly council, the role of the prophets and the council's ultimate fulfillment in Christ and the Church.)

God's methodology for warfare is found in Ephesians 1:17-19:

...that the God of our Lord Jesus Christ, the Father of glory, may give unto you a spirit of wisdom and revelation in the KNOWLEDGE OF HIM [the Christ], *having the eyes of your heart enlightened, that ye may know what is the hope of His calling, what the riches of the glory of His inheritance in the saints, and what the exceeding greatness of His power to us-ward who believe, according to the working of the strength of His might* (ASV).

Paul is communicating to the saints here that the antidote to the malicious activity of the gates of hell is the Spirit of revelation. Many commentators agree that although the word "spirit" is not capitalized in most translations, it refers to the Spirit of God, who is the Spirit of revelation.

The enemy works to intercept the knowledge of the Christ, to cut off that knowledge and to keep the Church in ignorance. Paul clearly states that the way to lose the cosmic battle is to remain in ignorance: "...that no advantage may be gained over us by satan: for we are not IGNORANT of his devices" (2 Cor 2:11 ASV).

Our General is not far removed from us, but fights with us on the front lines. He is with us always, even to the end of the age (Matt. 28:20). Christ has an objective that He came to fulfill, and He continues to work toward it in His present ministry as High Priest over a new nation. That objective is to accomplish the Father's eternal purpose. "...And to make all men see what is the DISPENSATION [points of development, increase and manifestation], of the MYSTERY which for ages hath been hid [undiscovered] in God who created all things..." (Eph. 3:9 ASV).

In actuality, Paul is groping for words to express what he is preaching. In this Ephesian passage he is making clear that to preach this MYSTERY is to preach the UNFATHOMABLE. In other words, it is utterance beyond articulation! It would be similar to making a mandatory broadcast in a large auditorium with an inadequate public address system. The word for "unfathomable" in verse 8 implies that it is untraceable. Our fellowship with Christ is therefore fellowship in a MYSTERY. The mystery had been hidden for centuries in the heart of the Father, and has now been revealed.

What was hidden in the Old Covenant? Was it the coming of the Christ (1 Sam. 2:10—the ANOINTED)? In Genesis 3:15 we know that the seed was expected and in Deuteronomy 17:15 that

17

the PROPHET was expected, and we also know that the KINGDOM would come (Ps. 89:4; 2 Sam. 3) and that the GENTILES would be brought in (Is. 42:6).

When Jesus faces His imminent death in Jerusalem, He is painfully aware of the wrong perceptions of Him that the crowds hold. He is aware that He has been rejected by the religious authorities over Jerusalem. In asking the disciples, "Who do you say that I am?" He is leading them to realize that they need to apprehend Him as the Son of God by the Spirit of revelation. As was stated already, that can happen only by an operation of the Spirit. It is a SEEING that is an ENCOUNTER, not unlike Isaiah's vision in the temple (Is. 6:1ff.). That SEEING, that ENCOUNTER, that REVELATION, is a CRISIS point in growth and maturity. Saul of Tarsus, in Acts 9, undergoes the same crisis. As with Simon Peter, so it must be with Saul and all of the saints.

The Spirit must show us the light of the glory of God in the FACE of Christ (2 Cor. 4:6). Paul, more than any other apostle, seems to articulate this message in its depths. Therefore, it behooves us to understand what Paul saw when he looked into the face of Christ. He tells us in Ephesians 1:16 that God was going to SUM UP ALL THINGS IN CHRIST. The concept of summing up deals with bringing back and reuniting around the main point. Something was dis-united, or dispersed, that Christ came to reunite. He is the pivotal point of that summing up; therefore, to see Him is to see the purpose of God and participate in the summing-up process. He came to seek and to save "that which was lost" (Matt. 18:11); that concerns much more than individual salvation. In the fullness of times everything will be regathered to Christ. Because alien forces oppose the eternal counsels of God, they resist the summing up of all things in Christ. The Scripture seems to indicate that as we approach the consummation, there will be a maturity both in the direction of glory and in the direction of chaos. It should not surprise us then, as believers, that the more we grow in the grace of Christ, the more we experience opposition from the powers.

The summing up of all things in Christ is the objective of the Father. It is the objective of the opposition to prevent that from happening. Although the foe is defeated, he is still deceived into thinking he can pull off his objective. The specific reason for the opposition of the enemy to the Church is the Church's unique relationship to the APPOINTED HEIR OF ALL THINGS. We are the ELECT of God and, as a result, will share in the inheritance of the Son. Election relates more to the purpose of God than to mere individual salvation. Warfare relates to purpose and destiny. To gain the superiority over the heavenly "air," we must by a revelation of the Son, in the Spirit, gain superiority over the lies we believed in our minds. "A wise man scaleth the city of the mighty, and bringeth down the strength of the confidence thereof" (Prov. 21:22 ASV).

CHAPTER THREE

THE UNEXPECTED EXODUS

And while He was praying, the appearance of His face became different, and His clothing became white and gleaming. And behold, two men were talking with Him; and they were Moses and Elijah, who, appearing in glory, were speaking of His departure which He was about to accomplish at Jerusalem (Luke 9:29-31).

The key to all the other miracles in the life of Jesus is found here in the account of the transfiguration.

After His discourse on the Church, the Kingdom and the keys, Jesus makes it evident that none of it could transpire except He die in Jerusalem at the hands of sinners. The concepts of the Messiah that the twelve disciples had were not that different from their contemporaries who rejected Him. It was scandalous to Simon Peter to think that Jesus the Messiah should be killed. However, the glories of which He spoke could not be entered into without the death of the Lamb of God. The Lamb of God must be slain in order for the Christ of God to be made alive. This too is an aspect of the undiscovered Christ in us with which we must deal. Nothing in us welcomes death. Everything in us resists it. In the order of God, however, death is the gateway to new life. Grief is the open door to newness. Until something old is taken away, something new cannot be given (Job 1:21)!

It is while Jesus prays that something happens to Him. His appearance changes from the inside out. He is robed in brilliant light. The parallel for this occurrence is found in Exodus 24:12-18, where Moses went up the mountain and was enveloped in the Shekinah for six days, and then heard the voice of the Lord. It is significant that this transfiguration should occur, and that God should come again, as He had done in ancient Israel, and put His glory on the face of a Man. Moses is the Old Covenant prophet who pre-figures Jesus. As Moses was endowed with the Shekinah glory after six days of waiting on Horeb, so now six days after the dialogue in Caesarea Phillipi and after Peter's confession, Jesus is enshrouded in the Shekinah glory on the height of a mountain. As all Old Covenant prophets would be in the image of Moses the prophet, so all New Covenant believers would be invested with the image of Christ. To be in the image of Christ is to be in the image of God. As Moses imparted his spirit to the seventy (Num. 11), and in particular to Joshua (Ex. 33:11), so too will Christ impart His glory to the disciples, and to the three on the mountain in particular. As Moses gives his spirit to Joshua and also to the seventy, Jesus will impart His Spirit to the disciples and then to the nations. In that sense, He is the father of a new race. He will beget sons in His image as Adam begat Seth in his image (Gen. 5:1-3).

In the account of Jesus' transfiguration, "two men" appear with Jesus. The fact that it is "two men" connects this portion of His life with the Resurrection in Luke 24:4 and the Ascension in Acts 1:10, where "two men" also appear. In the transfiguration account, however, these are not angels. Instead these are, perhaps, the two most significant figures of the Old Covenant. These are Moses (the embodiment of the Torah) and Elijah (representative of the prophets). These appeared in His glory. Jesus is to be heeded as pre-eminent over Moses and Elijah, because He is the proper interpreter of all that the law and the prophets represented. He came to complete all that they spoke.

Interestingly, Luke records for us what Matthew and Mark do not: the conversation between these three men. They spoke of "His departure" (Luke 9:31). The Greek word is *exodon*, from which we derive the word "exodus." Moses worked an exodus event out of Egypt. Elijah had his own exodus event by way of the chariot-throne of God east of the Jordan. What all these things have to do with the undiscovered Christ is important. There must be an exodus out of the old in order for there to be an entrance into the new. Jerusalem had become a "den of thieves." The multitudes were distressed and downcast, like sheep without a shepherd (Matt. 9:36).

The Hebrew concept of a shepherd was that of a king. Not unlike king Pharaoh, Herod was a taskmaster and a murderer (Ex. 1:22; Matt. 2:16). The failure of kings to be what God required and demanded according to the law is evident throughout Old Covenant history.

When you enter the land which the Lord your God gives you, and you possess it and live in it, and you say, "I will set a king over me like all the nations who are around me," you shall surely set a king over you whom the Lord your God chooses, one from among your **countrymen [brothers] you shall set as king over yourselves; you may not put a foreigner over yourselves who is not your countryman [brother].** *Moreover, he shall not multiply horses for himself, nor shall he cause the people to return to Egypt to multiply horses, since the Lord has said to you, "You shall never again return that way." Neither shall he multiply wives for himself, lest his heart turn away; nor shall he greatly increase silver and gold for himself* (Deut. 17:14-17).

The text goes on to instruct that the king is to write for himself a copy of the law of Moses in the presence of the priests and meditate on it daily lest he think of himself as better or greater than his brothers.

Most of the kings in Israel violated this commandment. As a matter of fact, Solomon, in all of his splendor, represents the epitome of failure. After the Queen of Sheba leaves his presence, he commences to commit all three of these sins and falls away from God. In Second Chronicles 9:13-28 we have the tragic account of a man who appears in natural glory, but who violated the covenant of

Jehovah. Consider the fact from verse 13 that in one year he collected for himself a large amount of gold, to the tune of 666 talents in weight.

It is appalling to read some of the erroneous interpretations of Revelation 13:18, in light of what John used as a referent. This number, this "mark of the beast," is man's attempt to arrive in glory by flesh and flesh alone. Yet man is a trinity of sixes and can never have a seventhth day of rest by accumulating wealth, political power (marrying daughters of foreign kings to avoid war) or military might (horses). Man must learn that it is "not by might nor by power [an army], but by My Spirit..." (Zech. 4:6).

It was the wise men who asked, "Where is He who has been born King of the Jews?" (Matt. 2:2). Moses had forewarned the generation in the wilderness of the challenges and issues they would face once they received the gift of the land. The responsibility of managing and stewarding the land was to be paramount in their minds in order for future generations to enjoy its benefits. When the nation repeatedly failed to heed the words of Moses in this regard, and kings went from bad to worse, God raised up men to bring the issues to the forefront and to call the people to account. Hence, men of old like Elijah began to address land rights. Jezebel, a foreigner married to an apostate king, abused the law and reinterpreted it to justify the murder of Naboth. Elijah, who stood in the heavenly council (1 Kin. 17:1), declared the judgment of covenant violation: for three and one half years it would not rain.

The implications were clear: Moses had brought the people out of the brickyard of Egypt, out of bondage to abuses of power, and into the liberty of shared and managed inheritance. Every man was to be able to have his own vine and fig tree (Mic. 4:4) and to enjoy the blessings of God. Moses' entire mission was to motivate the people to leave the world of Pharaoh for a new world made by the God of freedom. Centuries later they forfeited their freedom by abusing the land and one another. The alternative was clear: they would be expelled from the land and be brought back to bondage as they were in Egypt. Jeremiah was unpopular for his message, but Babylon was the destined place of judgment for the apostate nation. So Elijah had ushered in a breed of prophetic order that would, with signs and wonders, seek to call the people back to proper perspective.

The weariness of the journey and the mind-set of a generation born in slavery proved to be too great for Moses in the final analysis. His anger prevented him from leading the people into the land. The Lord Himself buried Moses' body in the land of Moab, and no one knew his burial place (Deut. 34:6). Jude tells us that at the time of Moses' death, satan argued with the archangel Michael (Jude 9) over his body, but failed to obtain it. What was the reason for the conflict? It is the same reason behind the conflict over the revelation of the Christ in the Church. If satan could inhabit the body of Moses and come back as Moses resurrected, he could interfere with the ongoing purpose of God, turn the people back to the opposite direction and destroy them altogether.

Elijah's departure also came at a time of weariness. He felt isolated and alone in his battle against the priests of Baal. He was angered by the apparent absence of others to stand with him. In his depression he lost sight of the larger picture. When brought back to Horeb, the mountain where God's glory was revealed to Moses, God sought to revitalize the prophet. Yet even in commissioning Elijah to three new tasks, (anointing Hazael as king over Aram, Jehu as king over Israel and Elisha as prophet in his place), he fails to follow through. He manages to anoint Elisha, but that is as far as it goes. The chariot-throne catches him up to glory and he departs from the scene (2 Kin. 2:11).

These two men, great as they were, typify the failure of the law and the prophets to perfect and raise up a community under a righteous king. However, consider the greatness of the grace of God in

28

choosing two who had been heroes in their own lives and yet who departed without ever completing their original tasks. These two are appointed by God to prepare Jesus for His EXODUS. His departure, however, will be radically different. Jerusalem, the once holy city, had become a harlot. John, in the Book of Revelation, typifies it as Egypt and Sodom (Rev. 11:8). It was a house of slavery, bondage and wickedness, full of spiritual adultery.

In order to bring a new nation into a new land, there must be an exodus event. It is Moses and Elijah who prepare Jesus for His departure. None saw Moses die, except perhaps Joshua, since it seems that they were together at all times. None saw Elijah depart, except Elisha. But all would see Jesus die on the garbage heaps outside the dung gate of Jerusalem. He would die the death of a criminal in the eyes of all who cared to observe. His death would not be pleasant, but horrifying. Yet unlike Moses, He would not utter threats against the rebellious, He would only offer forgiveness. He would love even to the end. Although even the twelve forsake Him, He would not be angered. He would rule His own spirit (Prov. 26:32).

Is it possible that Moses, in ministering to Jesus on the mount of transfiguration, is the acknowledgment of his inability to be complete without the Christ? What Moses failed to be in his latter days,

Jesus will prove to be before God and man. Likewise Elijah, who typifies resurrection (yet in an incomplete fashion), is the acknowledgment of the prophetic order's inability to accomplish the task of bringing corporate resurrection unless the Spirit that is on Elijah becomes a Spirit that indwells Elijah. Christ will be He who dies in glory and who arises again in glory. Hallelujah!

Jesus, the King at birth, reminds us that inheritance results from the grace of the Lord. Flesh and blood cannot receive the Kingdom. It must be by a work of the Spirit in the heart of man. Man must have an exodus event. Resurrection is the end of the three-day journey out of Egypt. What begins on the night of Passover as a meal in the midst of death, ends in a doxology of praise early on the morning of the first day of the week. Resurrection is the doorway into a new inheritance. Calvary is the place of departure from the old Jerusalem, the old order. The garden tomb on Sunday morning is the gateway to a new world where righteousness, peace and joy in the Holy Ghost dwells! What the dwellings of Israel on the eve of the Passover heard were the shrieks and cries of those touched by the death angel. Yet in the morning, on the other side of the Red Sea after the drowning of Pharaoh, what was heard was the beating of tambourines led by Miriam, as for joy they sang that "the horse and his rider" were thrown into the sea!

Christ gave Himself for the Church. He loved the Church so much that He died for her liberation from the brickyard! At resurrection, the seed of immortality was replanted into humanity (2 Tim. 1:10).

The glory that was present at the transfiguration was resurrection glory. The Spirit within us that heals and transforms us is the same Spirit which resurrects! This Spirit transcends death (Rom. 8:11).

How far has the church today drifted from the understanding the early church appreciated regarding the Spirit of Christ? The key to the existence of the fledgling church was the experience of the indwelling Spirit of Christ. The Day of Pentecost brought a new reality of the Spirit to the early church. Consider for a moment First John 4:1-3:

> Beloved, do not believe every spirit, but test the spirits to see whether they are from God; because many false prophets have gone out into the world. By this you know the Spirit of God: every spirit that confesses that Jesus Christ has come in the flesh is from God; and every spirit that does not confess Jesus is not from God; and this is the spirit of the antichrist....

John uses the aorist tense in this passage when he says "every spirit that confesses that Jesus

Christ HAS COME in the flesh." The aorist tense implies an ONGOING EVENT: past, present and future. God was in Christ as the once-and-for-all Incarnation. But John is not speaking of Jesus, the Man, here. He is speaking of the ongoing incarnation of Christ in the flesh: His Body, the Church, the fullness of Him who fills all in all! Anyone who denies that Christ is in the Church, that is, in the believers, is antichrist! Can we comprehend the magnitude of this fact? The Church is His Body, His ongoing presence in the earth. (I will speak of this concept in greater detail later on.)

It is for this reason that our understanding of the indwelling Spirit is so important. When the Church received the fullness of the Spirit on the Day of Pentecost, they understood that they had received the Spirit of the ascended Jesus. That meant they had received the firstfruits of the coming age. Paul reminds the saints in Ephesians 1:14 that the coming of the Spirit to empower the Church was a GUARANTEE, A DOWN PAYMENT, AN EARNEST DEPOSIT, of the inheritance to be expected in the future!

One of the great tragedies of our day has been the way we took the experience of the Spirit, withdrew from the world and consumed it upon ourselves. We ignored the larger issues. The Spirit of the risen Christ empowers us to touch the world.

Yet, for many, the world is outside the doors of our spiritual ghettos. Sadly, much of the popular sensational forms of eschatology, which peddle an erroneous view of reality and encourage us to look forward to an any-minute rapture, have contributed to the paralysis of our limbs. The Body of Christ is like the lame man at the Beautiful Gate in the temple described in Acts 3. We behave more like beggars than like priests of a better covenant. Dispensationalism is a Christ-less message and is not the gospel at all. How far we have fallen from the understanding of the early church and of the early church fathers on these issues! We've allowed our fears of social Darwinism and secularism to induce us to form and fashion a system of eschatology that saves us from facing reality. We have consigned the world over to evil and have allowed it, by our retreat, to consider us a non-threat to its transformation. The Spirit is in the Church to transform the world! Such was the view of the great apostle Paul, as well as of the other writers of Holy Writ, including the prophets of old. Such was the belief of Augustine, Polycarp and the like. Such was the conviction that led Martin Luther and other reformers to radically shake the generation in which they lived.

How far we have fallen! In the years since the Spirit invaded on the Day of Pentecost, men have institutionalized Him. The Roman Catholic Church has called the Spirit "the Soul and the Sustainer of the Church." What church? The Roman Church? Can the Spirit of Christ be institutionalized? The Protestants have declared that the Spirit is the One who justifies and awakens the individual to salvation and sanctification. Is the Spirit now only individualized? How tragic! God released His Spirit to indwell the Church in order for the Spirit to be the agent in the earth that moves all of creation to its consummation. The Spirit was given at Pentecost by the ascended Christ for the purpose of leading the Church, and in so doing lead the creation to its ultimate destiny, which is the summing up of all things in Christ!

The event of Pentecost very clearly meant that the new heavens and the new earth had already begun. Why? A NEW MAN was in the glory! Mary's boy, one of us, made a radical departure from the Adamic race and caused an exodus event. He laid hold of the keys of death, hell and the grave. He led captivity captive. He cleansed the heavenly sanctuary by His own blood. He sat down as a Man. That was a never-before event! There was a Man in the glory. The new heavens were instituted at the Ascension. Pentecost was also a never-before event! On the Day of Pentecost, the new Man in the new heavens released the newness of His Spirit to the earth. The faithful 120 followers, who awaited this newness, were not disappointed on the Day of Pentecost. They were part of the new earth God was producing by the indwelling Christ!

This Church, this ongoing incarnation of the Christ, by the Holy Spirit, acts creates and shapes history and leads creation to its final goal. The life-giving Spirit of the ascended Jesus has been released in the earth through the Church. It is for this reason the Church can rejoice with the psalmist when he says, "Thy people will volunteer freely [will be free-will offerings] in the day of Thy power" (Ps. 110:3a)!

CHAPTER FOUR

THE UNDISPUTED KEYS

I will give you the KEYS of the kingdom of heaven... (Matt. 16:19).

Keys to the kingdom are promised to Peter as well as to the rest of the disciples. It is important, however, to emphasize that there is an order revealed in our text. Let's just review that order for a moment.

1. "Thou art the Christ." One must see Jesus as the Eternal One, the Heavenly One, who predates existence.

2. "You are Peter." When Simon sees beyond the humanity of Jesus and sees the Heavenly and Eternal One, Jesus is then able to "see" beyond the Simon-nature and "see" the nature of his image in God. Simon is the man after the flesh; Peter is the man after the Spirit. Man cannot be transformed from his Adamic inheritance until he beholds a new face and a new image. That new image is in Christ. Simon, in seeing Christ, is liberated through the revelation of Christ to see a new man in himself. Christ affirms the new nature and gives Simon a new name equal to that nature. But Christ in Peter is different from Christ in Paul. "Christ in you" is that unique expression of the Son of God that no other shares, since you were uniquely created to bear His image. When Simon saw Jesus in His proper context by a revelation of the Father, Jesus was free to reveal to Peter what God saw of him in his proper context.

3. "Upon this Rock." The revelation that He is the Christ is the rock-solid foundation upon which the "called-out ones" are built.

4. "My church." The Church is His Church; therefore, it is His possession. We cannot build it; only He can. May God deliver us from trying to build what is not ours to build!

5. "The gates of hell shall not prevail" (KJV). Regardless of the conflict that follows the revelation of the Christ, we are guaranteed ultimate triumph over all of the wiles of the enemy.

6. "I will give you the KEYS of the KINGDOM." Here we come to the verse in question. The giving of keys is predicated upon the understanding and the experience of what went before. The KEYS are the sixth element in this divinely ordered sequence. Although I am not called to build His Church, (only He can do that), I am called to extend His Kingdom. In order to extend the KINGDOM, Jesus makes it clear that it is necessary to possess the KEYS. If we are to understand what these KEYS really are, and we need to, then perhaps the best approach is one of careful study and inquiry as to where, prior to this occasion, KEYS are mentioned in the Scripture.

Isaiah sets the tone for Jesus' commentary to Peter: "Then I will set the KEY of the house of David on his shoulder, when he opens no one will shut, when he shuts no one will open. And I will drive him like a peg in a firm place, and he will become a throne of glory to his father's house" (Is. 22:22-23). This passage in Isaiah is typological of the Christ, although it refers to actual persons in the prophet Isaiah's day. Eliakim, which means

"God will affirm," will be a servant to the Lord and a father to the community of Israel, unlike Shebna (whom Eliakim will replace), who abused power and lorded it over the flock of God. Eliakim would be accepted both within and without the royal court. In the New Covenant, Jesus was affirmed by God at His baptism and accepted by some in the royal court of Herod as well as by many outside it, both Jews and Gentiles.

Eliakim also would be given the "key of the house of David." This phrase appears again in Revelation 3:7 when John says that the ascended Christ has the KEY of David. The understanding of the Hebrew community was that whoever had the key of David was authorized to open and shut the royal court of the king to whomever he desired. The possessor of the key was empowered to grant entrance and exit, access and egress to and from the throne room and all the royal chambers. All business transacted in the royal household was in the hands of he who had the key. In the Scripture, the key of the "house of David" in particular had a prophetic implication relating to the Davidic kingdom. Please note also from this passage that the key is on Eliakim's shoulder. That obviously is tied to Isaiah's previous prophecy from chapter Isaiah 9: "For a child will be born to us, a son will be given to us; and the government will rest on His

40

SHOULDERS..." (v. 6). Shoulders relate to government. The priests of the Lord carried the Ark of God on their shoulders. So Eliakim was granted a place of high honor and esteem in the Davidic monarchy.

Jesus applies this reference both to Himself and to those who recognize Him as the Christ, the Heir of David's throne! At one time Simon did not have any access to the royal court of Heaven. But the Father of the Lord Jesus, by the Spirit of revelation, opened his eyes to see the Christ of glory veiled in the flesh of Jesus. At that crucial point, the heavens were opened in a new way for Peter (the new man in Christ). That point of access, granted by the Son and approved by the Father, gives the new man opportunities to look in the royal court and to get involved in the royal affairs of the King. Up to this point he has been excluded, although still part of the commonwealth of the King. Now he has been granted access. Christ is the place of entry. He is the door.

That is the same thing Jesus endeavored to share with Nathaniel when He said, "Truly, truly, I say to you, you shall see the heavens opened [literally split wide open], and the angels of God ascending [access] and descending [egress] upon the Son of Man" (John 1:51). Notice, Nathaniel too will have the privilege of the KEYS of the KINGDOM. Also take note that ascent and descent into the heavenly court is tied to the revelation of the "Son of Man." More than any other title, Jesus refers to Himself as the Son of Man. Thus His own understanding of who He was in His humanity is essential to our insight into Him as the undiscovered Christ. Where did Jesus develop a consciousness of His role as the "Son of Man"? Consider Daniel 7:13-14:

> *I kept looking in the night visions, and behold, with the clouds of heaven One like a Son of Man was coming, and He came up to the Ancient of Days and was presented before Him. And to Him was given dominion, glory and a KINGDOM, that all the peoples, nations, and men of every language might serve Him. His dominion is an everlasting dominion which will not pass away; and His KINGDOM is one which will not be destroyed.*

Within the context of Daniel 7, the sovereign God removed the authority of the "beasts" that rule the world and judged them. He then gives all the authority and dominion to this Champion and Hero, referred to as the Son of Man. The destruction of the world powers in the first part of Daniel's vision is not the end of the whole vision. He "kept looking." That ought to serve as an important lesson for those of us who become preoccupied with the rise and fall of world leaders and oppressors.

The Church must keep looking for the Son of Man. So what ends as the destruction of the world powers in the vision marks the commencement of the building of the foundation of the KINGDOM of God by the Son of Man! The clouds in the vision represent the glory in which the Almighty dwells. It is a GLORIOUS and HEAVENLY KINGDOM! This KINGDOM will know no end! HALLELUJAH!

Daniel tells us that he saw one "like" the Son of Man. Why does he say "like" the Son of Man? He did so for the simple reason that he saw the preincarnate Christ. He was not yet in the flesh as Jesus. He was in His preincarnate glory. The humanity of Christ was not present from the beginning of time. Although liberal theologians take issue with WHO this figure is, the best interpreter is Jesus Himself. He clearly refers to Himself as this Son of Man (Matt. 25:31; Mark 10:45; Luke 17:24; etc.). This Son of Man is no mere mortal. He is a person of supernatural origin and dimension. He comes with clouds of glory and has access to the royal court and to the throne, and an everlasting and universal KINGDOM is given to Him. Yet in Daniel's vision, this One is also seen in His humanity. It was in His own person and work in the flesh that He thus obtained the eternal KINGDOM.

What a marvelous promise given by Jesus to both Peter and Nathaniel. Those who come to know

Him by revelation as the Christ of God, the Son of God, would participate in the heavenly court. They would be granted access to the royal chambers and could conduct business on behalf of Heaven. Jesus understood this promise in His own life, even from the time of His youth. It was after His bar-mitzvah at the age of twelve, when He became, according to Jewish custom, a "son of the law," that He began to articulate His understanding of His own destiny in relation to the heavenly purpose. "Did you not know that I had to be in the affairs of My Father?" (Luke 2:49).

These marvelous KEYS provide immediate access to resources which, up to this point, were hidden and unknown to the disciples of Jesus. It is important for us to develop this thought of access a bit further here in order to secure it in our understanding.

> *Thus says the Lord of hosts, "If you will walk in My ways, and if you will perform My service, then you will also GOVERN MY HOUSE and also have CHARGE OF MY COURTS, and I will grant you FREE ACCESS among these who are standing HERE"* (Zech. 3:7).

This passage of Scripture is in the middle of a vision that concerned the high priest Joshua, who represented the nation of Israel in the presence of

Jehovah. Once he is cleansed of his filthy garments (literally, garments covered with dung), he is redressed in new vestments. Simon is the old nature, clothed in filthy garments. At the gracious revelation granted him by God in recognizing the Christ, he is redressed as Peter, a new man. The vestments worn by the priests of old liturgically represented the hopes of the people to one day be dressed in the glory of heavenly splendor. The vestments were also colorful and vibrant, and represented that the people would one day suddenly be absorbed in the wonders of God. For the high priest to be granted free access among those (the angelic council; please understand that is why HE is called the Lord of the HOSTS), who stand HERE, we must realize that HERE is the heavenly court, the royal throne room. The promise was presented to Joshua the high priest for divine intimacy and for access to the celestial council chambers.

The marvelous application of this promise for Peter, the disciples and us is this: Under the old economy, only the prophets had access to the heavenly council. But here in Matthew 16, Jesus reveals a divine order and then promises the entire Church that, if we will apprehend it by grace, we will have access to the council chambers of the Most High and walk in a level of intimacy the prophets of old never had, even in their wildest dreams! Listen to what Jesus says to these common folk: "For truly I say to you, that many prophets and righteous men desired to see what you see, and did not see it; and to hear what you hear, and did not hear it" (Matt. 13:17).

There is one other example worth pondering. In John 3, Nicodemus, a Pharisee, a teacher of Israel, who "knows" the law, comes to Jesus by night. John lets our imaginations become riveted to the picture here. One can only see shadows at night. In the dark, nothing is clear. So too, while it is nighttime in the natural, Nicodemus lives in the night in his inner being. Reading in the dark is almost impossible. Seeing in the dark is equally impossible. A veil is over the eyes of Jews, Paul tells us in Second Corinthians 3, at the reading of Moses. Nicodemus is in the dark about Jesus. The only thing he cannot figure out is how Jesus can do miracles if God is not with Him. The Savior gets right to the problem. He lets Nicodemus know that he suffers from "night vision." "Truly, truly, I say to you, unless one is born again, he cannot SEE the kingdom of God" (John 3:3).

Nicodemus struggles to understand the metaphor Jesus uses here. His "flesh and blood" rabbinical education blinds him from SEEING. His training has darkened, rather than enlightened, him. Jesus clearly causes the disciples to understand that the letter kills, but that the Spirit gives life.

Nicodemus is trying to figure out how he can be reborn. He is on the right track, but in the wrong arena. Can a man enter his mother's womb a second time? Before you say "No, it's impossible," it would serve you well to be freed from your "flesh and blood" thinking. Jesus speaks of heavenly reality, but Nicodemus is thinking in earthly terms. The answer to Nicodemus' question is YES! You can reenter your mother's womb a second time. As a matter of fact, it is essential. The question is not "How can it be done?" The proper question is "WHO is my MOTHER?" If one were to ask Nicodemus who his father was, he would answer with either his birth father or Abraham, his father in the faith. Jesus, we know, had arguments with the Pharisees as to who their father was. In John 8:44, the Pharisees claim Abraham as their father, but Jesus says quite emphatically that the devil is their father. Apparently Jesus never read Dale Carnegie's *How to Win Friends, and Influence People.*

Jesus is in a different mode in His dialogue with Nicodemus. Nicodemus is being led to raise questions, indicating that his heart hungered for the truth. He merely needs some help in transferring out of his darkened understanding into the light of God's grace. For Nicodemus, learned as he is in Holy Writ, the Book is a closed Book. He was, at that time, living in a world of darkness.

If Abraham is his father, then his mother must be Sarah. The significance is that God brought life from a barren womb. The seed of Abraham, the child of promise, the laugh of faith, is birthed by a barren womb. Out of the pain of Sarah's barrenness was born a nation. It was the pain of being childless that led to being impregnated with the life of God! "Listen to me, you who pursue righteousness, who seek the Lord: look to the rock from which you were hewn, and the quarry from which you were dug. Look to Abraham your father, and to SARAH who gave birth to you in pain..." (Is. 51:1-2). To return to the mother's womb a second time is to be made aware of man's inability to produce an understanding of the Christ. It is always the barren womb from which prophetic newness is birthed. "But the Jerusalem above is free; she is our MOTHER. For it is written, 'Rejoice, barren woman who does not bear; break forth and shout, you who are not in labor; for more are the children of the desolate than of the one who has a husband" (Gal. 4:26-27).

Nicodemus must realize that "flesh and blood," the finest rabbinical schools in Jerusalem, cannot give him access into the KINGDOM of God. In order to gain access into the KINGDOM, he must be granted access by the KING who has the KEYS! Jesus makes it evident that Nicodemus must be born of water and of the Spirit in order to gain entrance into the royal court. That cannot happen except by a WIND that blows unhindered by "flesh and blood." What is the WATER? This word would obviously stir up in the mind of a teacher of the law a picture of the LAVER in the outer court of the temple, or tabernacle. To be "born of the Spirit" would relate to entrance into the Holy Place, wherein dwells the lampstand, the table of shewbread and the altar of incense. Yet for all this knowledge, Nicodemus is still in the dark. He still has not gained access. Jesus heightens the frustration of this ruler of the Jews and even uses irony when He says, "Are you the teacher of Israel, and do not understand these things?" (John 3:10). What vexation of mind and spirit. Poor Nicodemus! To make matters more complicated, Jesus then refers to all that He had just discussed, namely, being born again, water baptism and baptism of the Spirit, as EARTHLY. These things relate to functioning in the EARTHLY arena (v. 12). He says, "If I told you earthly things and you do not believe, how shall you believe if I tell you heavenly things?"

I wonder if we as the church of the end of the twentieth century can hear this discussion as addressed to us? Can evangelicals, mainline denominationals, Baptists and Pentecostals hear this message? Is Jesus saying that, even after you understand what it is to be born again, even after you are water baptized, even after you are baptized in the Spirit, you are still only in the EARTHLY ARENA? Can the ascended Lord tell the twentieth century church heavenly things, or will we still argue over our pet doctrines? For all our arguments, we are still only touching EARTHLY and individual issues. What about the greater issues? What about the destiny of the nations and the summing up of all things in Christ? Do we really understand what the KEYS of the KINGDOM are? Do we really know CHRIST? Or is He yet UNDISCOVERED? What of the destiny of every tribe, race, kindred and tongue? What of the authority to change the course of human history by having access to hidden information held by God in the holiest of all, for any who is willing to be delivered from "flesh and blood"?

Can Jesus tell us heavenly things, or are we still asking the wrong questions? Listen to Him: "And no one has ascended into heaven, but He who DESCENDED from heaven, even the Son of Man" (John 3:3). Did you read that verse correctly? Jesus says "ASCENDED" in the past tense. He does not speak here of His ascension after His resurrection. That event has not happened yet. Instead He metaphorically speaks of access into the celestial court by the Spirit while in prayer and in meditation. When in communion with the Father, He

SEES and HEARS things in the HEAVENLY COUNCIL CHAMBERS, and operates in them when He DESCENDS back into the world of fellowship with men. He lives in a place of access and egress in relation to Heaven's courts. He lives a balanced and integrated life. He lives life as God intended for man to live it. Life is lived in an integration of the heavenly with the earthly. Life is lived as a participation with God and the heavenly council, who operate through humanity and by His Spirit in the earthand to bring about His purposes.

It seems as though we have been guilty of the worst kind of reductionism. As stated previously, we have institutionalized as well as individualized the Spirit. We pray for "our needs," or for "our church," while His Church goes unnoticed. To touch the heart of God and to affect the affairs of the nations seems a bit out of reach for many of us. We are consumed with survival. We haven't the time or the desire for heavenly things, or eternal things. In the West in particular, we have become enculturated into a value system that runs counter to the KINGDOM of God. We may not be so very different from the exiles in Babylon, who grew comfortable in Babylonian culture and never returned to their homeland. Why? The price they would have to pay to rebuild the walls of Jerusalem was too high a price, and too enormous a task, to guarantee that nothing would disillusion them.

Jesus, the Son of Man, lived a fully integrated life. He lived in the "ascending and descending" pattern of the angelic council of old. He, the Christ, learned obedience through what He suffered in this regard. Yes, much could have disillusioned them. Yes, much can disillusion us. Nevertheless, what Jesus said to Peter is as good a promise today as it was when He spoke it: "I will give you the keys of the KINGDOM..." (Matt. 16:19). Christ, the KING, has KEYS to give to our generation. It is His will to give us access in the celestial court. He desires us to be with Him on a level of intimacy that we have never known. He makes us to know that much of Him is yet UNDISCOVERED! He extends those KEYS to transformed men and women. He extends those KEYS to Simons who, by SEEING CHRIST, have become Peters! Is He extending the KEYS to you, beloved? Will you receive them?

CHAPTER FIVE

THE UNEXPENDABLE SECRET

...and whatever you shall bind on earth shall have been bound in heaven, and whatever you shall loose on earth shall have been loosed in heaven (Matt. 16:19).

What a powerful impartation of power and authority. In the Talmud, the concept of binding and loosing deals with prohibiting and permitting. It referred to both things and actions. It also has connotations of remitting or pardoning. Binding and loosing also concerns legislative as well as

judicial power. Rabbis had this authority under the
tradition of the elders. They had the authority to
declare certain acts as lawful or unlawful. They
also had the authority to declare a person guilty or
not guilty, and could either hold them liable or free
them from punishment or compensation. (For a
more detailed explanation, see *Life and Times of
Jesus the Messiah* by Edersheim, p. 361).

All the necessary functions that apostolic ministry were to assume was granted here to the
Church; first to Peter, as representative of the
twelve, and after Jesus' resurrection to the rest of
the disciples (John 20:23). The power to retain or to
forgive sins is the subject on which John focuses in
his Gospel. The reason is his concern with the concept of community. Matthew's account seems to
allow for other issues in binding and loosing. For
Jesus, these were concepts that He realized the disciples would not grasp immediately. Neither do we,
2000 years later, grasp them immediately. Matthew takes careful thought in expressing this
learning process: "Now when Jesus came into the
district of Caesarea Philippi, He BEGAN ASKING
His disciples..." (Matt. 16:13); "From that time
Jesus Christ BEGAN TO SHOW His disciples..."
(Matt. 16:21). These truths, once revealed, must be
reiterated constantly before the disciples could
grasp the implications of them. The proof is Jesus'

rebuking Peter after their dialogue about His death in Jerusalem (v. 23).

Jesus intends to reproduce Himself in these His nucleus and to empower them to fulfill the destiny of the early church. Isaiah describes the Christ in this fashion: "Behold, My Servant, whom I uphold; My Chosen One in whom My soul delights. I have put My Spirit upon Him; He will bring forth justice to the nations" (Is. 42:1). Jesus is chosen and elect by the call of God. So too these who are with Him are chosen and elect by the call of God. Jesus is endowed with the Spirit of the Lord; they too are promised the same endowment (John 14:16). He embodies a full range and scope of knowledge of the counsel of the Lord and "binds and looses" accordingly: "A bruised reed He will not break, and a dimly burning wick He will not extinguish; He will faithfully bring forth justice" (Is. 42:3).

Jesus possesses the Spirit without measure and is commissioned, or apostolized if you will, from the heavenly council to establish a new covenant by becoming the LIVING PROPHETIC WORD of God. Jesus the Christ manifests the glory of the only begotten Son of the Father, and He is the Builder of the Church and Ruler of the Kingdom as King-Priest of a heavenly order that exceeds the Aaronic priesthood. Aaron had authority to bind and loose in the earthly arena. The New Covenant priesthood, after another ORDER, a HEAVENLY one, has authority to bind and loose in the heavenly arena, in cooperation with the divine, heavenly council. This Heavenly Man desires to have a company of saints in His likeness who can officiate as His king-priests here on the earth. Not only is it His desire that through legislative and judicial authority this company of saints would extend His Kingdom, it is part of the foreordained counsel of the Lord.

Consider the following passage: "Blessed be the God and Father of our Lord Jesus Christ, who has blessed us with every spiritual blessing in the heavenly places in Christ [please note that "places" is plural; there are progressive realms of authority in the heavenlies], just as He CHOSE us in Him before the foundation of the world..." (Eph. 1:3-4). The word Paul uses when he describes our election in Christ is "chose." The Greek word for CHOSE is *eklego*. Paul emphatically stresses the inevitable, indisputable, sovereign and eternal purpose of God. The word *eklego* is translated "to pick out, to choose." The stem of the word indicates "the telling over." The word itself is made up of two words: *ek*, meaning "out of," and *lego* (a derivative of *logos*), which means "to speak." The word encompasses three ideas: the first is the "speaking forth" or the "telling over," the second indicates the rejection of some and the acceptance of others and the third indicates "the talking to Himself" (see *Linguistic Key*

to the Greek New Testament, Reinecker & Rogers).
In other words, God was talking to Himself and
speaking forth the elect long before creation was in
existence.

Are we prepared to accept what Paul is declar-
ing? Before God said, "Let there be light," He had
already spoken forth the elect! We are not derived
from apes or amoebas. As a matter of fact, we are
not even derived from the creation. Creation is
lower in rank to humanity. We were spoken out of
the mouth of God prior to creation. In other words,
Christ is the *logos* of God, the sum total of all that
God is, the TOTAL DISCOURSE of GOD; yet the
Church was spoken forth, *eklego*, in Christ
BEFORE THE FOUNDATION OF THE WORLD.
The truth is, Christ is THE WORD, but you are "a
word" from God in Christ! Romans 8:29 lets us
know that we were foreknown in eternity past in
CHRIST!

What we need to realize is this: Simon was
named by his birth parents as Simon. That is who
he was in time and space. However, he was Peter in
the mouth of God (God talking to Himself) before
the foundation of the world. This concept is
prefigured for us in the Pentateuch in Genesis
32:27-28: "So he said to him, 'What is your name?'
And he said, 'Jacob.' And he said, 'Your name shall
no longer be Jacob, but Israel....' " Jacob was the

name and label given to him by Isaac and Rebekah.
Israel was the person God spoke into existence
before the foundation of the world! This knowledge
ought to give us confidence in our place of Christ as
the Church. As a word in the mouth of God prior to
creation, I ought to rejoice and rest in the power of
God. Contemplate the following verse of Isaiah in
light of Paul's statement in Ephesians 1:3: "So shall
My word be which goes forth from My mouth; it
shall not return to Me empty, without accomplishing what I desire, and without succeeding in the
matter for which I sent it" (Is. 55:11). Perhaps we
also need to give John 15:26-27 a new hearing in
light of this truth: "When the Helper comes, whom
I will send to you from the Father, that is the Spirit
of truth, who proceeds from the Father, He will
bear witness of Me, and you will bear witness also,
because you have been with Me from the BEGIN-
NING." Can Jesus be attempting here to make the
disciples aware of their election from before the
foundation of the world? It is certainly reasonable
to assume so.

Let's go back now to a scripture we considered in
a previous chapter and make the application to it.
Ephesians 3:9 states: "and to bring to light what is
the administration of the mystery which for ages
has been hidden in God, who created all things."
We must ask ourselves what Paul saw, in the face of

Christ, that previously had been hidden. The Church was certainly not hidden, for in the Old Covenant, the "congregation" of Israel existed. The key verse is, perhaps, Galatians 3:28: "There is neither Jew nor Greek, there is neither slave nor free man, there is neither male nor female; for you are all ONE [literally, ONE PERSON] IN CHRIST JESUS." "For even as the BODY is ONE and yet has many members, and all the members of the BODY, though they are many, are one BODY, so also is CHRIST" (1 Cor. 12:12). What Paul saw, which was hidden in the eternal counsels of God, is that the Church was Christ's BODY. The Church was CHOSEN in CHRIST, "spoken forth" in Christ prior to creation. Our existence in the mouth of God pre-dates anything in the natural order. We are His BODY! As the HEAD is CHRIST, so the BODY is CHRIST!

Of course PETER would have the KEYS of the KINGDOM. Of course PETER has authority in the earthly and in the heavenly to bind and to loose. PETER was foreordained and foreknown by God. Peter was CHOSEN in CHRIST as part of the BODY, the fullness of Him who fills all in all! (See Ephesians 1:23.)

The first man, Adam, is built from the dust; the second Man, Jesus, is the *logos* come from Heaven. Adam the first man was of the earth; Jesus the second Man is from Heaven. The principle can now be applied to the Church, His BODY, the NEW MAN of Ephesians 2:15. This NEW MAN will grow to be the MATURE MAN of Ephesians 4:13. Simon had no power to bind or loose. Simon was of the earth, built of the dust of Adam. Peter, however, the man of the new creation, is of Heaven. He is part of the Corporate Heavenly Man. Paul assures us that if we have borne the image of the earthly, we shall also bear the image of the heavenly (1 Cor. 12:49).

All distinctions, other than Christ, are non-existent. There is neither Jew nor Greek, slave nor free, Barbarian nor Scythian; ALL are ONE PERSON, ONE NEW MAN, ONE BODY in Christ! We are ONE NEW RACE! And if we are to have authority to bind and loose as was promised, we must realize that the Greek tense implies that one can bind on earth only what has ALREADY BEEN BOUND in Heaven. One can loose on earth only what has ALREADY BEEN LOOSED in Heaven. When were things bound and loosed in Heaven? May God help us to understand this truth and elevate us to a new level of joy unspeakable and full of glory.

"Known unto God are all His works from the beginning..." (Acts 15:18 KJV)! God was finished long before we ever started. It is essential for us to gain access to the celestial court and to inquire of the heavenly council, for that is where all things have been bound and loosed. It is in that arena where, when we ascend to the hill of the Lord, we see all the things that God has prepared for them that love Him. It is there they are revealed by the Spirit (1 Cor. 2:10). Paul tells us that these things have already been prepared. In the eternal decrees of the Almighty, it has already been done.

This knowledge, however, by no means leaves us without anything to do. That which has been decreed in the heavenlies must be echoed in the earthly if it is to be manifested. Jesus said that when we prayed, we needed to say, "Your kingdom come. Your will be done on EARTH as it is in HEAVEN" (Luke 11:2 NKJ). If there is no Peter to stand in the earthly and declare what has been decreed in the heavenly, it will not be done! We cannot bypass the exercise of faith in these matters. Faith is a call to action! Christ will not move apart from His Church, His Body, operating in faith and calling those things that are not as though they were. Faith has substance and weight precisely because faith SEES in the invisible and brings to pass in the VISIBLE. The worlds were framed and structured by the Word of God. So too, on the Day of Pentecost, the history-making Spirit of God came to indwell the Body. Therefore, when the Body speaks out of what it SEES in the celestial courts, and speaks it in the created world, transformation occurs. The divine fiat is expressed through the mouth of the Church.

One more comment bears mentioning. Judgment has already been written against every principality and power. The princes and powers have already been sentenced to execution. Why then do they prevail in the earth? Two passages of Scripture bear consideration. The first is Daniel 10:21: "However, I will tell you what is INSCRIBED IN THE WRITING OF TRUTH. Yet there is no one who stands firmly with me against these forces except Michael your prince." The prophet Daniel has a terrifying vision and is overwhelmed by it in this chapter. Much of what is learned refers to the end of the age.

In the vision, the pre-incarnate Christ comes to make Daniel aware of the warfare taking place in the heavenlies regarding the nations, as opposed to the nation of God. The Son of God makes it clear to Daniel that the demonic princes have already been written about in a book in Heaven, and sentence has already been passed. However, the Son of God had battled those princes in direct response to the prayers of Daniel. The tragedy was that His coming to Daniel was hindered for 21 days. Why? Although the hosts of warring angels under Michael, as the chief warrior angel, stood with the Son of God on behalf of Israel, He clearly states that no one else besides Daniel was showing himself strong in the earthly arena to bring about the desired victory. If successful warfare is to be waged, Christ needs a BODY in the EARTH that will stand strong and declare what has already been decreed in the heavenlies. It matters not what God has decreed; there must be agreement on the earth with what has been foreordained in Heaven.

Could Jesus be referring to this concept when He makes the statement, "Now shall not God bring about justice for His ELECT, who cry to Him day and night, and will He delay long over them? I tell you that He will bring about justice for them speedily. However, when the Son of Man comes, WILL HE FIND FAITH ON THE EARTH?" (Luke 18:7-8). It would seem that when the pre-incarnate Christ "came" to Daniel, HE DID NOT FIND FAITH ON THE EARTH (other than Daniel). This passage cannot be relegated merely to Jesus' second coming. There is given to us here a KEY, if you will, a principle related to divine visitation and to divine vindication. That KEY is this: For whatever is happening in the heavenlies, there must be an earthly counterpart mirroring the same thing. Sometimes this principle lies hidden in Scripture and at other times it comes to the forefront. Many "comings" of the Lord, besides His final second coming, are in Scripture. When He comes to us by the Holy Ghost in the midst of individual, corporate or national conflict, does He always find faith? The answer is obvious. He does not. We give up too quickly. We grow weary too easily. We grow disillusioned too frequently.

This principle of binding what is already bound and loosing what is already loosed can be seen in Ezekiel 1:19-21:

And whenever the living beings moved, the wheels moved with them. And whenever the living beings rose from the earth, the wheels rose also. Wherever the spirit was about to go, they would go in that direction. And the wheels rose close beside them; for the spirit of the living beings was in the wheels. Whenever those went, these went; and whenever those stood still, these stood still. And whenever those rose from the earth, the wheels rose close beside them; for the spirit of the living beings was in the wheels.

The picture here is an appropriate one to describe the concept "whatever you bind...shall have been bound." The Body must move in symmetry with the Head. We must coordinate our movements with Him. Wherever He goes, we must go also. May the Christ of glory raise up a willing people in this day of His power; may we grasp these truths and apply them to our corporate life.

Let's look at one final passage as we conclude this chapter, found in Psalm 149:6-9:

Let the high praises of God be in their mouth, and a two-edged sword in their hand, to execute vengeance on the nations, and punishment on the peoples; to BIND THEIR KINGS WITH CHAINS, and their nobles with fetters of iron; to execute on them the JUDGMENT WRITTEN [Written where? In the heavenly council and the eternal decrees of God]; *THIS IS AN HONOR FOR ALL HIS GODLY ONES. PRAISE THE LORD!*

CHAPTER SIX

THE UNHINDERED HOPE

I thank my God always concerning you, for the grace of God which was given you in Christ Jesus, that in everything you were enriched in Him, in all speech and all knowledge, even as the testimony concerning Christ was confirmed in you, so that you are not lacking in any gift, awaiting eagerly the revelation of our Lord Jesus Christ, who shall also confirm you to the end, blameless in the day of our Lord Jesus Christ. God is faithful, through whom you were called into fellowship with His Son, Jesus Christ our Lord (1 Cor. 1:4-9).

The Church has been called into *koinonia*, fellowship with the Son of God. The concept of *koinonia* deals with participation. Whatever the Son is doing, we are to be doing with Him. Paul refers to this interaction in Philippians 2:1 as "participation in the Spirit" (RSV). This marvelous reality of "participation" in the Spirit serves the purpose of God for the Church in many ways. It would be an understatement to say that with all these lofty and grand concepts of Christ, the Church, the keys, the Kingdom and legal and judicial authority, the Church is still at times wounded, hurting, bleeding, in error or in sin. We live in a world that is fallen, and it seems as though change takes a long time. Even in our own individual lives, those "little foxes" in our personalities don't change overnight. Since we indeed wrestle with principalities and powers (Eph. 6:12ff.), and since it is a corporate wrestling ("we"), there must also be corporate comfort and fellowship.

The Body needs to be enriched continuously in speech and in knowledge (experiential knowledge) of the Christ. This fellowship is with One who is eternal in His existence, His Sonship and His anointing. We must come to know Him who was from the beginning (1 John 2:14).

The Church came into existence by a dynamic encounter with the Christ. Christ has become salvation for the Church. He then gives "ascension gifts" (Eph. 4:11), and comes to us through them in didactic fashion, teaching us the way to apply what we have come into. But He also sends to us the Comforter, the Paraclete, the Spirit who comes alongside us, dwells within us and makes us a COMMUNITY in the fellowship of the Son. It is the Spirit who in His activity in the Body makes us to know that our "here and now" situations matter to God, and that God cares. The Spirit makes real to us that we are part of God's new creation and have been included in His new beginning. It is the Spirit of Christ who calls us to live in the love of God and in the fellowship of the Son.

The participation to which we are called in the Body is what it is because the Body is the environment where life can truly bud and blossom and where the individual can realize his or her full potential.

The ancients were looking for the "consolation of Israel" (Luke 2:25). When Simeon held Jesus in his arms, he realized that the consolation of Israel was the Christ. Even though still a babe, the Christ consoled the aged Simeon. Simeon was comforted by the Christ. Fellowship with the Son brings comfort. There is a difficulty, however. The difficulty lies in the fact that our concepts of comfort fall short of the biblical concept of comfort. The Paraclete, the Comforter, the Holy Ghost, and His presence in the Body has been at times limited by our preconceived religious traditions and by our tendency to reduce

Scripture to what we assume it says, rather than comprehend what it really tells us. The concept of comfort is not foreign at all to the Old Covenant. As a matter of fact, in the Septuagint, which is the Greek version of the Old Testament, the Greek word for comfort appears quite often along with a second, equivalent word. The synonym for "comfort" is a word that means "to relieve" or "to cause to breathe again" (see *Dynamics in Pastoring* by Jacob Firet, Eerdmans Publ.). This word assumes a pre-existing state of pressure and anxiety.

When "comfort" comes, relief from the pressure comes. People no longer suffocate under the pressure, but can breathe freely once more. It's not unlike the commercial on television that asks, "How do you spell relief?" Redemption is, for Israel, the greatest expression of comfort. When the Redeemer returns to Zion (Is. 52:9), comfort is given. Comfort is that power which draws people out of distress (see Firet, *Dynamics in Pastoring*, p. 72). David says, "This is my comfort in my affliction, that Thy word has revived me [preserved me alive]" (Ps. 119:40).

Isaiah 40:1 says, "Comfort, O comfort My people...." This word is given as a command. N.H. Smith, in his book *The Distinctive Ideas of the Old Testament*, says the following:

The command, "Comfort ye" does not mean that consoling words are to be spoken to one in the midst of sorrow in order that the sorrowful one may continue bravely in the tribulation. It means that words are to be spoken which will MAKE AN END OF SORROW, and so will comfort OUT OF sorrow and not IN SORROW.

When true comfort is given, situations and perspectives change. When the Comforter comes, things change! When we participate in true fellowship, true *koinonia* with the Son, by the Spirit, things do change!

Job experienced frustration with his "friends" because their "comfort" had no worth. Their words did not bring him out of his distress. As a matter of fact, their words continued to suffocate his spirit (Job 16:3). Isaiah describes what should have happened in the "community of Job": " 'I have seen his ways, but I will heal him; I will lead him and restore comfort to him and to his mourners, creating the praise of the lips. Peace [*shalom*], peace to him who is far and to him who is near,' says the Lord, 'and I will heal him' " (Is. 57:18-19). The biblical concept of *shalom* is a continual vision of joy, harmony, well being, health and wholeness, prosperity and protection. It consists of well being in the midst of and in spite of surrounding dangers or threats to security. It is not some ethereal utopia, but rather wholeness right in the midst of every imaginable evil that could assail the community of God. It is a level of peace and well being that is more than individual; it is for the corporate community.

Our call to fellowship in the Son is a call to this kind of well being and wholeness in the midst of tribulation and warfare. The community of God, the Body of Christ, is called to nurture *shalom*. We are called to "comfort." We are called in the fellowship of the Son to nurture God's hope. That *koinonia* produces, as we read in our opening text, an "enriching in Him" as well as an eager anticipation of a fresh revelation of Him, and the impartation of gifts in the service of Him (1 Cor. 1:4-7). Christ in us is the hope of glory (Col. 1:27). The scriptural concept of hope is far different from the whimsical and wishful thinking of fallen humanity. Hope in Scripture is properly defined as "desire married to expectation." As the community of Christ, the Spirit, or the "Comforter," has been given to work through us to nurture the indwelling Christ in one another. In our fellowship in Him, by the Spirit, we are to continually edify one another and build one another up, thus stirring up the indwelling Desire (the Christ) coupled with eager expectation that He will deliver us out of our sorrows, tests, afflictions, trials and difficulties.

Therefore having been justified by faith, we have PEACE with God through our Lord

Jesus, through whom also we have obtained our introduction [ACCESS] *by faith into this grace in which we stand; and we exult in HOPE of the glory of God. And not only this, but we also exult in our tribulations, knowing that tribulation brings about perseverance; and perseverance, proven character; and proven character, HOPE; and HOPE DOES NOT DISAPPOINT, BECAUSE THE LOVE OF GOD HAS BEEN POURED OUT WITHIN OUR HEARTS THROUGH THE HOLY SPIRIT WHO WAS GIVEN TO US* (Rom. 5:1-5).

CHAPTER SEVEN

THE UNSILENCED CRY

To him who overcomes, I will grant to eat of the tree of life, which is in the Paradise of God (Rev. 2:7b).

This fellowship with the Son, to which we have been called, is, as has already been stated, a participation with Him in His affairs in the earth and the heavens. Both in the letter to Corinth and in this promise to the overcomer in the church of Ephesus, there is something we need to realize. The truth is, when these glorious statements and promises were made, what was threatening the *koinonia* was already there. The forces of chaos were already at work in Corinth. Paul also expressed concern in his departure from Ephesus, that great center for revival. He said that after his departure, savage wolves would come in and cause disintegration (see Acts 20:29ff.).

It is imperative that the church of our day and age realize the grave importance of the fellowship of Christ. Satanic forces have been unleashed in unprecedented fashion and at times we are painfully ignorant of it all. This revelation of Christ in the Church is what the forces of chaos most fear. This revelation represents the greatest evidence and ultimate reality of their defeat. Their objective, therefore, is to keep us thinking individualistically. If the enemy can get us on grounds other than the corporate Christ, our effectiveness is neutralized.

There must come a return of glory to the LOCAL CHURCH. The idea of a "mystical body of Christ" is foreign to Scripture. The prevailing secularism of our day has fostered an attitude of religious humanism in the church that manifests itself as "What's in it for me?" That ought not be the question we ask. Although we benefit greatly from the blessings of covenant and although community life meets the needs of the people, when functioning properly, the real question we must ask is, "What's in it for Christ?"!

We are to be a corporate expression of resurrection power. Our apathy toward involvement in corporate worship and faithfulness in coming together has its roots, not in the need for "personal space," but rather in the strategy of the powers of darkness to keep the Church from being a testimony of resurrection life.

The local church must not become just another meeting place, but a ladder into the heavenlies. It must become a sanctuary of glory where angelic hosts hover and usher in the Wind of God. We will not produce disciples by making legalistic demands to fulfill traditional obligations. Ministry must be under a divine mandate to preach the Christ. When we must resort to demanding commitment, it is evident that we have lost the glory!

When glory is on a people, the hungry will come. The drawing power of the ascended Christ is unlimited in its scope. It requires no program or format, no gimmicks or manipulations. It requires only a deep hunger and desire for the manifestation of His glory! It requires a revelation not only of Christ the Head, but of Christ the Body. If we would but ask the Spirit of God to give us a revelation of the Church as He ordained it to be, it is most likely that we would never need to encourage people to come together in the spirit of unity and love. If the eyes of our understanding were enlightened to see the Church as Christ sees it, attendance at corporate gatherings would not even be an issue.

Is the Holy Spirit satisfied with a "remnant theology" so prevalent in many circles today? Is that the plan and purpose of God? Or have we used the concept of a remnant theology based on the behavior of an apathetic church? Have we held out and spelled out clearly enough the vision of what is in the heart of the Father? Or do we merely touch it at a surface level, and thus say "peace, peace" where there is no peace? Have we only medicated the pain in the hearts of the disturbed? When I speak here of the disturbed, I speak of those who are disturbed over the lack of the fullness of the glory in the Church. We have become numb to the ache within us. The Spirit has placed a divine ache in the heart of the Church. That divine ache is a "deep calling unto deep."

Asaph cries out, "When I remember God, then I am disturbed" (Ps. 77:3a). At the remembrance of the God of glory and at the awareness of His power, might and ability, Asaph cries out from the pain of the present sense of powerlessness felt by both him and the community of God. Have we lost a hunger for the tree of life? Have we replaced that hunger with programs and organizational structure? Have we medicated a pain that was put in the heart of the Church by God? Is there a pain in the Church that was given as a GIFT? Has the Spirit changed? It was the travail of the Son of God that brought forth the New Covenant community! It was the labor pains of the Christ that birthed the new thing! If the Spirit always begins in pain and travail, why medicate the pain? If there is a tree of life, if there is a paradise of God, and if we are not partaking of it, why deny it or mask it? Why pretend we are when we are not? Why heal the wound of the daughters of Zion slightly? Why tranquilize the Church from its holy anxiety? If glory is absent, we must not numb the pain. We must face the pain. Pain is an indicator of something UNDISCOVERED and UNDETECTED within us! Pain is a teacher that leads us to ROOT ISSUES.

Paul cries out from his pain over the Galatian church when he says, "My children, with whom I am again in LABOR until Christ is formed in you" (Gal. 4:19). The heart of Paul is what the apostolic and prophetic heart should be for the church today. Have we replaced Christ with a formula or a program? Have we fragmented Him into little pieces and lost sight of the WHOLE CHRIST? The church at Ephesus, with all its growth, splendor and teaching, had lost its first love. It was in danger of losing its light and of having its lampstand removed. Were there within that congregation a group of saints who at one time remembered eating at the tree of life in the paradise of God? Where are those people now? Will those people overcome the complacency and pride that made them secure in their success or in their knowledge and rediscover the Christ who is the Tree of Life?

Jesus clearly states that mourners will be blessed. It is mourners who receive comfort (Matt. 5:4). Remember, the biblical concept of comfort is deliverance out of sorrow and a change of situation. Prophetic grief and travail is the gateway to newness. Radical newness will not emerge from "creativity," as in the sense of brainstorming, unless that brainstorming results from recognizing that the old things failed. Otherwise creativity becomes merely rearranging old things into a new configuration. If the furniture in your living room is so old that it is worn out, no matter how many ways you arrange it, it still will not comfort you when you sit on it. Although the arrangement of the furniture may be new, the furniture is still old and has outlived its usefulness. The furniture might have cost a great deal when it was purchased. When it was new, it was glorious. But after years of wear and tear, it has lost its ability to be comfortable.

Many times in the history of the people of God, there have been methods effective for the generation they served. Yet they eventually outgrew their use-fulness. The Ephesian church began as a thriving and pulsing body, a living organism, but by the time John writes his letter to them from the risen Christ, it had become nothing more than an organization with structure and program, but NO PASSION.

Partaking of the tree of life is a promise given to the overcomer. Overcomers are those who overcome the tendency of the community to forfeit passion for sobriety. Overcomers are those who choose Christ rather than religious activity. Overcomers are those who remember what they once had and, with prophetic understanding, mourn over its loss, become disturbed over static conditions and ultimately receive comfort from Christ. As Christ travailed and prophetically mourned to birth the new thing in the earth, so too the Body must enter into His suffering and afflictions and by the Spirit give birth to a fresh manifestation of the Christ in this generation!

Jeremiah cries out, "O that my head were waters, and my eyes a fountain of tears, that I might weep day and night for the slain daughter of my people!" (Jer. 9:1). Jeremiah was called to preach a message that was not only unpopular, but also rejected as a lie. In essence, Jeremiah's message was that Jerusalem, as Israel had known it, was coming to an end. God was going to pluck up and break down, destroy and overthrow and then build and plant. Although Jeremiah was by his words to execute the judgments of God on the nations, his words were first directed to the "secure and safe" world of Jerusalem as it was known. The glory had long since departed from it. So God would take away the old to establish the new. Unlike the kings and princes who rejected this word, it was Jeremiah and the weeping women who responded properly. When the king could not face the end of Jerusalem as he wanted it, Rachel wept (Jer. 31) on his behalf.

Spirit-led grief is prophetic. Rachel, a dead woman, was still weeping for her children. Rachel, the barren woman, wept until she gave birth to Joseph. She also wept in the birth of Benjamin. His birth cost her, her life. She named him "son of my sorrow." Jacob changed his name after she died. It was the travail of Rachel again that faced the end of an old regime when Herod could not embrace the change. Herod did not want to face the end of his domination (Matt. 2:16ff.). In his failure to embrace God-directed change, he failed to face the pain of his secure world coming to an end. As a result, he destroyed a portion of the new generation. A dead woman was heard crying down through the ages of history. Rachel was once again weeping for her children. As a generation of children was being murdered and denied its destiny, a barren woman cried again for the birthing of a new generation. The Church must, in a Spirit of Christ, like Rachel, weep for those that refuse change. We must weep for those who destroy a portion of the new generation in their selfishness and unwillingness. Yet also in the tradition of Rachel, the Church must weep out of its barrenness for the birthing of a new generation and for a fresh revelation of the Christ.

"To him who overcomes, I will grant to eat of the tree of life, which is in the Paradise of God." (Jesus)

CHAPTER EIGHT

THE UNENDING ANTHEM

Now to Him who is able to do exceeding abundantly beyond all that we ask or think, according to the power that works within us, to Him be the glory in the church and in Christ Jesus to all generations forever and ever. Amen (Eph. 3:20-21).

Here Paul climaxes his thoughts on the eternal perfections and purposes of God and bursts forth in a hymn of celebration and praise ascribing unending and unlimited power to God the Father. It is his doxology of the *dunamis* of God. In modern vernacular, it could be called a doxology of dynamite.

Paul is making it clear that the purposes of God in Christ will ultimately prevail throughout all generations by the dynamite of God. The Spirit of God in the Church, the indwelling Christ, is the dynamite of God. That dynamite, that explosive power, lies within us. That dynamite, Paul says, works within us. The divine ability to do it all is in the Body of Christ.

Paul also affirms the goodness of God in these verses. That is right and ought to be so. As we consider, in this last chapter, the final applications and implications, we must see it as the culmination of all we have been considering. We have looked at the power of prophetic grief and have grasped the fact that the doorway to new things is often travail and pain. "...The Lord gave and the Lord has taken away, BLESSED BE THE NAME OF THE LORD..." (Job 1:21). In other words, the locus of praise, the doxology of praise, is birthed out of grief and loss. Something is removed, something is lost, and we learn to grieve the loss in order that through the process of grief, we are prepared to face life anew and receive new gifts from the God who continually surprises us with new things. One cannot sing a doxology of dynamite except one has first sung a dirge of destruction. It is out of our losses that we find our greatest gains. It is in letting go that we find life.

We must affirm that, throughout all the transitions Christ brings the Church, He is ABLE. Indeed, He is ABLE. Every generation that connects with Christ is able to affirm His wonder-working power and ability.

Numerous references to His great ability are in Holy Writ, but let's remind ourselves of just a few of them.

And God is ABLE to make all grace abound to you, that always having all sufficiency in everything, you may have an abundance for every good deed (2 Cor 9:8).

For since He Himself was tempted in that which He has suffered, He is ABLE to come to the aid of those who are tempted (Heb. 2:18).

Hence, also, He is ABLE to save forever those who draw near to God through Him, since He always lives to make intercession for them (Heb. 7:25).

For this reason I also suffer these things, but I am not ashamed; for I know whom I have believed and I am convinced that He is ABLE to guard what I have entrusted to Him until that day (2 Tim. 1:12).

This Christ cannot be defeated. The Body cannot be defeated. No sin can withstand His power; no sickness can withstand His power. Neither satan nor the gates of hell can thwart His power. Not even death can hinder or resist His power. The Christ of glory is ABLE to meet the needs of the Church, to deliver us from all manner of evil, to keep us in perfect peace, to enlarge us in our distresses, to soothe us in our fears, to comfort us through our afflictions and to keep us from falling. What a mighty God we serve!

Nothing can hinder the dynamite of God from accomplishing the purpose of God in the Church, EXCEPT you! This power of Christ, this One who indwells us and nurtures us can be released by only one way. It must be by what Andrew Murray called "the cauterizing power of the Cross." The cross must ever be active in the inner life of the Church. We must KNOW this UNKNOWABLE ONE. Like Paul, we must journey by way of the cross through the loss of all things (Phil. 3:8), in order to gain the surpassing value of knowing Christ. At the end of his life, this great apostle, who seemed to know Him better than any other, cries out:

That I may KNOW HIM, and the POWER **[dunamis]** *of His resurrection and the fellowship* **[koinonia]** *of His sufferings, being conformed* **[by way of the inward cross]** *to His death; in order that I may attain to the resurrection from the dead.*

Not that I have already obtained it, or have already become perfect, but I press on in order that I may lay hold of that for which also I was laid hold of by Christ Jesus. Brethren, I do not regard myself as having laid hold of it yet; but one thing I do: forgetting what lies behind and reaching forward to what lies ahead, I PRESS ON toward the goal for the prize of the upward call of God in Christ Jesus (Phil. 3:10-14).

We must come to know this UNDISCOVERED CHRIST both in height and in depth. There are four dimensions to experiencing truth. The Church must comprehend all four dimensions by the power of the Holy Ghost. The Church must embrace all four-dimensions in order to be whole. Interestingly enough, Paul, in Ephesians 3:17-18, gives us the four dimensional knowledge that must be comprehended. We must know the BREADTH, LENGTH, HEIGHT and DEPTH! In meditating on this passage of Scripture, please notice the ORDER in which that four-dimensional awareness is given. Depth is the last of the four dimensions. Depth, the deep inward working of the cross, is both the end and the beginning for the Church.

Knowledge of Christ can be gained only by the Spirit doing a work deep within the heart of the

Church. The Father will reveal the Son to whom He wills. That revealing will be an inward work of grace. The Father is pleased to reveal His Son IN THE CHURCH and IN THE BELIEVER (see Galatians 1:16). May we, as the community of God, be pleased to allow Him to do so. May we come to know the unexplored regions of this UNDIS-COVERED CHRIST!

THE INNER DIMENSION

by *Mark Chironna*. In order to fulfill
our destiny, we must decide to move
on with God, a decision that is made
in what Chironna calls "The Inner
Dimension." TPB-126 p.
ISBN 0-914903-24-1 Retail $4.95

TO ORDER: CALL 1-800-722-6774
Also available at your local Christian
bookstore